The Problem
With Drinking

The Problem
With Drinking

Poems

○○○○○○○○○○○○○○○○○○○○○○○○

Knicholas Kennedy

Knicholas Kennedy is a current college student studying computer engineering. He spends his free time reading novels, drinking, and debating the usage of the Oxford comma. He is an aspiring novelist, and you may find him traveling the country – hoping to meet you.

The Past is a man in a barb wire suit waiting to say hello

maybe every pain
you have ever experienced
will echo
throughout your life

constantly calling you
back to a time
when you were less
than you are now

but maybe
that's all we are

just a series of stories
built of old hurts

and the person
we become
is just the best version
of ourselves
at ignoring
all of the suffering
we see around us

vernacular

your father taught you
how to break hearts
using empty liquor bottles
and letters to people
he would never send

your mother
showed you how
to run
when it starts
to hurt a little
too much

and they both
gave examples
of being too afraid
to be happy

so I guess
it was too late
for me to explain
the difference
between something breaking
and things
falling apart

hospitals

there are
entire hospitals
filled
with all of the things
that remind me
of you

like the thought
of a person waiting
in a window
for someone
who will never
visit

maybe
it is the sound
of a man
falling apart
when he is told
that the worst
is yet to come

it is found
in the sound
of a door closing
for the last time

dry storms

one day,
lightning will ignite
every part of your brain.

you will jolt
and wonder why
you didn't
see the storm
sooner.

van gogh

Van Gogh
saw too much beauty
too fast
and never got over it.

he was sitting
in a little room
when he looked out of his window
and saw the beauty
in a pale lamppost
sitting next to a single star
and needed to show
his brother
what that beauty meant.

so he took up
drawing
and painting.

he
wanted to·believe
that eating yellow paint
would make him happy.

he needed
to believe it.

you see,
Van Gogh knew
that's all any of us
are really doing

with our time.

drinking yourself to sleep –
trying to feel full of something.

calling your mother to say hi –
wanting to hear her say,
"I love you,"
the way she would
when you were a kid.

eating yellow paint -
hoping to be happy.

eating yellow paint
to be happy.

eating.
yellow.
paint.
to.
be.
happy.

and sometimes,
we run out of paint
or get sick
and die.

so eat it
while you can.

starsick

the sun
never asks permission
to kiss you
and the moon
never pretends
that it wants
to stay.

so when the sun
fell in love
with the moon,
I already knew
how it would end.

it ended with her
waxing
and waning
on my couch
at three in the morning.

it ended with the sun
telling me,
"I'm not the bad guy
here – she is.
She just
doesn't get me
and I got
so jealous."

I nodded my head
and agreed with both of them.

I drank
all the good whiskey
and listened to the sounds
of the universe
being miserable.

I nodded my sage-wise head
and thanked both of them
for confiding in me.

Now I knew
what not to do.

letter 1

I can't do this
anymore.

I've cared and cared
and cared,
until the world
broke
and was reshaped
in the image
of man.

I destroyed civilizations
of mad ideas
and insane opinions
in a dash
to win you back.

I even
ended a friendship
or four.

None of it worked.

Now
it is broken
and the clockworks
are grinding out.

the gears are stripped
and I don't know,
maybe I never did.

the sea to see

I never learned
to kiss a woman once.

it was like drinking
salt water to me -
the more that
touched my lips,
the thirstier I got.

my father taught me right.

coffee-stained story

I was sitting in a coffee shop
with Maggie
when we started arguing.

she was tired
of everything needing a meaning,
of me wanting a meaning.

Maggie wanted to be happy
just for happy's sake.

I told her I couldn't do it.

I told her I couldn't do it
over a sip of almost-warm coffee
and told her that there is always
a deeper meaning.

I asked her
what this was all about.

Maggie told me
with train track tears
running down her eyes,
"I lied about loving you
to make sure you
would never leave me.
I am sorry,
but I just don't
see the point."

I blew out a big sigh
told her it was okay
tried saying it was fine
but my hand
was clenching and
unclenching.

my heart
was beating too fast
and too slow.

my mind
was going over
every conversation
from goodbye
to hello.

so I stood up
and walked out on her
because I realized
the scariest thing about her.

she was right.

hope is a face passed on the street that you will never see again

all of my favorite people
are filled
with empty passions –
empty of humanity.

or overflowing with it.

straining at the edge
of a cliff face trapped
in a bag of shit
and blood.

and still more human
than anything else
I've ever seen.

and I see no stars
tonight
or any night.

they are shrouded
in clouds,
lighting the way
for better men.

the doctor

I took another bite
of the apple
today.

it was delicious
in ways
you can only understand
once you have
tasted it.

it should have been
our apple
but you said
you had never
tasted it
and that you
never would.

so I sit alone
taking bites
out of love
and wondering
what you have
always eaten.

it certainly
wasn't love
even if I
wish it had
been.

(sex, laughter, and secrets
are all
wonderful things
but there's a demon
in my bloodstream
and bruises
on my brain.

these are things
that you can't fix
and I don't love you)

attraction is mental

I wonder
if magnets
ever get lonely
because
they never
have anything
in common
with the ones
they are
attracted to?

arrogant

I have probably fucked
three or four
dozens of women.

some of them physically
all emotionally.

I have squandered
more love
than any man ever
has a right to.

I am too much
and not enough.

but women love
men that burn
and the brighter
the flame
the hotter
the fire.

wrinkles

I saw a man today
sitting on a bench
stone-drunk
and passed out.

people walked by
and said he must
have it so good
to be so drunk
and so happy.

but
they didn't
see his tears
or hear his fears
and everyone
only sees the bottle.

I am sad
and scared.

People are just
not good
to each other.

I asked him
about his name
and hat,
he started crying
and laughing.

some days it will rain

one day on my road,
I saw a little old
drunk
walking a brown pup
down the alley.

it was always raining then.

I remember how it
drenched him
and
his little brown
pup
but neither seemed rushed.

in fact,
a little comfortable.

the drunk
turned his head
away from his wetness
and laughed,
startling me,
and said,
"spend your time
in the rain.
this is how
life should be."

I took another
sip of whiskey.

sickly conditions

people pretend that art
writing and
music
are creative,
expressive.

Bukowski had it
right.

it is a form
of sickness,
we all
have something
that makes us
sick.

thoughts
that need to be
handed down,
put down,
and drawn over.

or else you die
just like everyone else
with an art condition.

love yourself
or whatever it takes
but drive it,
force it out,
kill it.

steak and eggs

the world
eats good men
for breakfast
every single day.

it is insane.

we pass up
chances to be
loved –
cared for –
appreciated.

all in the name
of sex
or something else
that is sex
in the way
that sex
never will be
sex.

love
is a fist
bled black
and blue.

sit down.

eat your breakfast.

roses

we accept
the type of love
that we
think we deserve.

it is why
your self-esteem
destroys you.

we only allow
what we believe
is deserving –
fair –
even.

And you
accepted
none of it.

your life is a burning tongue

women interest me
in ways
the rest of the world
never has.

some are sweet
and spoiled.

others come with fire
in their veins
and flames stuck in
the soft touch
of two hands touching.

and I love them
all.

it's stuck

this girl -
we can call her
Ashley.

she
is always bored.

bored.
bored.
bored.

it is so strange to me!

everything in the world
to see
and do
with the obvious answer
being that bored people
are boring -
but that must be a lie.

yes.

bored people
are dead.

Jesus
was bored
for those three days
and so
are you.

she came from movies and starlight

she came from movies
and starlight
to rest her weary head
upon the devil's lap.

no.

I'm sorry,
it's all backwards.

she was thirteen
the first time
her brother touched her.

fifteen
for her father.

mentally challenged
and raped by
dogs.

isn't the world
a beautiful place?

she had movies in her eyes
and stars in her words.

we learned from our friends

people mistake arrogance
for confidence.

it's why we fuck
the wrong people.

it's how
people can trick
attraction
or friendships
but get insecure
and drive people
out.

we trick ourselves
more often than not.

thump

I.
gave.
you.
a.
heart.
beat.
and.
all.
you.
did.
was.
complain.
about.
the.
noise.

novella

love
is a book
that has never
been creased
because
someone enjoyed it
so much
that they
simply
remembered the pages.

names

it's been
three years
and I
still
can't write
your name
without
poetry.

a crooked nose and a slanted smile

films and television
always taught me
that I would know my lover
by the curve
of their face
but I notice
the crook of their arm,
shape of the hips –
the stare in their eyes
when they are telling you
everything
that you never wanted
to hear.

heaven help us

if only every kiss
didn't burn like heaven
or freeze like hell.

if only every secret touch
didn't promise lust
or swear love.

if only it had been an angel
instead of a demon
to ask if I
was okay that night.

if only.

a god looks down
upon me
and says,
"though the rain
may wash away your sin
a devil is a devil
and you will not
see me again."

names (2)

my professors
taught me that
we could make anything
sound like poetry
but
I have been
saying my own name
all of these years
and I have yet
to hear
the rhyme scheme.

stutters and lisps

a man lets fear
step on his toes
rub his face
into the dogshit
and lie to him
every single day.

it controls his mind.

he is afraid to love –
of being loved –
of failing.

he is afraid that people
do not get better
and our lives
stop feeling okay.

so he goes mad
and madness
isn't a disease –
it's a cure.

it's the cure
for a world
that doesn't love you –
it doesn't love itself
either.

we have all done things
that we can't take back

and darkness
doesn't grow
it pulses.

it breathes it
lives inside of you
and doesn't die
until you do.

grand canyon quakes

there are cracks
through my brain
fault-lines
where sunlight
never wants to go.

because the sun
never forgave me
for teaching the world
what it meant
to live in the dark.

(You are a mushroom. A what? You
know, a mushroom – kept in the
dark, fed a diet of bullshit. Oh.)

snipping ropes

we live on a planet
where every single being –
every single creation
wants to hurt you.

survival
might not mean much
but I would rather
spit in their eye
than be grinded
under a boot.

never let them win.

never give in
to the idea that all of this
is too much –
too hard –
not worth it.

never let them look you
in the eye
and say that you
have lost
because survival
is the only way
to let them know
that you don't care
for their rules –
their way of life -
the ideas they put in you.

barflies

a bar crawl is what happens
when you put
too many stupid people
in a single area
and expect them all
to fall in the same direction.

expect them
to become sheep
in the name of the wolf
for at least
one night.

man.

a bar crawl
sounds pretty good.

rack

everyone always tells you
that pain
demands to be felt –
that there is one constant
in our lives.

pain.

I disagree –
I think that if you
take the legitimacy
away from something
then it becomes
marginalized.

it is just pain.

say it again.

it.
is.
just.
pain.

tell yourself this
between ragged breaths.

say it when you
are crying in the rain
and trying to forget her name.

believe in it - sure
pain exists
but dismiss it
as a petty thief
and it becomes
unimportant.

do this with everything -
with anything that bothers you.

that's enlightenment.

just remember -
the world isn't on fire
we are
and we burn lower
every single day.

friends

I used to spend hours
hunting my insecurities
through a brick house
that never felt like home.

I spent years with people –
family
or friends
approaching me
with hands held out wide
shouting at me,
"look what we found."

as if all any of us wants
is for every person you know
to bring your insecurities
back from windows and balconies –
dusty attics and dead basements.

they just go through your home –
your heart –
places of solitude,
heavy-handed,
drinking all of your problems
and swimming in discomfort
smiling as if it's a quirk
as if they will go away.

dreamers

I never learned to sleep.

I have nightmares
almost every single night
but I don't think they come back
because I'm not sure
that they ever really left.

they sit in the corner of my mind,
in every nook and shadow
waiting until it's just me
and him.

they know when to play
and when to fight.

they are constant companions
waiting for your brain
to die.

raincoats and paychecks

we live our lives
like so many puddles –
one small splash
and our calm
is completely shattered.

but with enough time,
rain and patience
we can each
become a lake.

beds are in hospitals too

another nightmare.

another night of me
sleeping like I need someone.

all curled arms
and closed knees.

tangled up in my sheets
like I'm hoping
you are hidden
in them.

another night
spent dreaming of people
that don't exist any longer.

bus tickets to anywhere

I will no longer allow
any sort of pass,
no tickets or free rides.

discounted rides are not allowed.

renting for the weekend?
forbidden.

I will not be shelved –
will not be stuck
in dreary attic storage
while collecting dust
until you are ready to use me
again.

I will become terribly worn –
well-used is the word.

you will choose me
every single day
or you won't get me
at all.

suicide and timesheets

I may not
have ever seen a woman
slit down both her wrists
but I have seen women drink
and drink
and drink
until their souls
are fit to burst –
filled with empty calories
and empty promises.

I may not
have seen a woman hang herself
but I have seen her
self-destruct over men –
drugs –
problems.

I have seen women
become human
and nothing was sadder.

untitled

I drink a little bit
at least once a day.

drinking problem?

there is no problem with this.

there is no sin here.

do not let the world
give you guilt and pain
over your vices.

let them find you
split belly open
for everyone to see.

alcohol kills
and cures.

now what it kills
and what it cures
are both
up to you.

a letter to my therapist

you never tried
to make me whole.

you never wanted me
to understand myself.

you didn't even try
to do anything
except make me happy
and what would I be
without my refrain?

pigeon

the world is an old man
screaming
that he will shit
on everything you love
and constantly
floating over your head.

searching for signs
that he can bother you
with a little more shit
and a little less rain.

closing time

salt spray and teeth
fill the air.

drizzling death
to a paper house
that smells of apathy
and garbage.

knowing that the sea
always returns to its own
we discovered our waters
were acid-tinged.

kissing corrosion.

whiskey

there is no reason
to dream
when you are always
sleeping.

so why stop to think
when you are always feeling?

just let it all happen.

everything.

all at once.

and breathe for once
goddammit.

ragged

one day the sky
will swallow all of your dreams –
your hopes,
the sorrows and pain.

and in the end
you will look up at the sun
and realize
that everything is beautiful.

maybe even pain is beautiful.

maybe especially pain –
it makes you who you are.

you don't have to understand
anything about it
to appreciate what it made you.

newspaper clippings and
lost conversations

I once stared a woman
too beautiful to approach
and a friend asked me
with a coy smile on his face
if I was afraid
to speak to her.

so I told him the truth –
that the only person
I have ever been afraid
to speak to
is God
and that I just wasn't sure
if they weren't the same person.

an apology I'll never send

so here we sit
like to old stones
sharing the last
dying rays of the earth.

radiant
from the heat of the day.

glowing
in a furnace
of shimmering air
but as the sun shifts
the forge grows cold
and so do you.

fuck or fight

I've seen women
faster to share a bed
than their hearts
and I'm sorry
but I knew I couldn't help.

it's not easy –
none of it is.

I've seen men
bent out and cold
destroy everything
they touch.

I need to believe
in what people can offer.

I want to so badly.

but how can anyone
with the world
the way it is?

Most days
it doesn't even flare
it just aches
and itches
and aches again.

it has to be heart burn –
it's just heart burn, right?

there is no way
that this is me
sitting in a corner
sobbing over someone else's
problems.

it's got to be indigestion –
no one gets like this
over sitting in a coffee shop
and listening to people
complain and complain
and hurt each other.

just
kiss me again
teach me how to do this
or at least
trick me into believing
that we aren't all alone
please.

pastures and gardens

I keep a garden
stuck deep in my chest
and I water her
with booze –
drugs –
hope –
whatever I like that day.

I water that garden
every single day
and I'm not sure
what I would do
without my vices.

probably
just let that garden
wilt.

quit fucking yourself

the reason
that there are so many people
is that humans
are meant to create.

art.

music.

literature.

and when we run out
of ideas to build
we create children.

everything was awful but we did it anyway

I did all of those terrible things
because I was afraid to do them.

it's the same thing we say
when we are too afraid
to jump a gap
shave our heads
or love someone else.

I did it because
I was afraid to do it.

It works
because everything
I have ever loved
scares me
at least a little bit.

click

I.
gave.
you.
a.
heartbeat.
but.
all.
you.
did.
was.
complain.
about.
the.
noise.

novels

love is a book
that has never
been creased
because you enjoyed it
so much
that you simply
remembered
the pages.

it is also a book
with every page creased -
ripped and teared
because you couldn't
put it down.

I am breathing too fast and nothing comes in any longer

you just don't get it.

bruises keep sprouting
from under my fingertips
whenever I touch her
and I tell her I love her –
- I really try to mean it
but the truth
is that I have always known
the hardest lies
we save for ourselves.

such as how
I have always stood
in front of every mirror
screaming incoherencies
about my too-tight ribcage
and how I don't love myself.

it is the way pavement cracks
under the weight of sentences
you are too afraid
to let go of.

it is why we bleed
when doing the right thing.

icebergs

I can still hear your voice
echoing throughout places
that we used to frequent
and I'll prove global warming
by showing everyone there is
how everywhere we have kissed
has become degrees hotter
so don't say you never loved me
your lips weren't meant for lies
they were made to melt icebergs.

untitled #2

I cracked my graveyards
wide open
and told her the truth –
that we always comfort people
with the words
we would want to hear ourselves –
that you can hear someone's heart
breaking
from giving others advice
they are too afraid to listen to
for themselves –
that we are each broken
in our own way
and that we are puddles
pretending to be lakes.

rain clouds
wishing we held
something more.

dentistry

my dentist
keeps finding pieces
of my past relationships
stuck between my teeth
and she's been asking me
what I've been trying to swallow
so I told her about the thoughts
that I've been chewing on
and I ask her if she thinks
it will affect my health.

she asks if it hurts to smile yet.

I tell her no –
that I hadn't thought it would.

she tells me,
it will soon enough.

with no clouds in the sky

the first night
we slept together
it poured so loud outside
that we forgot how to sleep
without our hands
finding a little bit of rain
underneath the blanket
with us
and so we made a storm
to keep us both awake.

seminar

when was the last time
that you placed hands
on someone else
and didn't leave them
with bruises
on every single place
that you decided to touch.

family

I miss you
every single day
the same way
that lightning strikes –
all at once
so that I stumble.

then I try to pretend
that I'm okay.

personal

it is in the crawl
of a semi-truck
going from zero
to sixty miles power hour.

it is in the slow,
sorry years
of a powerful heart
pulling
six-thousand pounds.

your eyes were the color of a storm in summer

I often think back
to that day
when you told me
that my eyes
were the color of hazelnuts
and wonder
if you had any problem
crushing me
with your hammering heart
or if everything
that you screamed
before you left that night
helped give you the strength
to do it
with your bare hands.

it grows cold

everyone always told me
I would eventually touch something
so hot
that I couldn't help but
end up burned
yet no one warned me
about the time
that I would hold a glacier
inbetween my arms
and whisper love to her
until I went numb.

snakes and toads

people always say
that women
words
and wine
can all be venomous
but I knew
that it was poison
for me to kiss her
because venom
has to be forced
into a victim
and I drank
every drop of her
willingly
even knowing
she would be
the death of me.

post card poem #1

one day in a world
so beautifully lit
you will meet a shadowed man
in a shadowed little bar
and you will start seeing the sun
as just another light
just as all of the night stars
will cross your mind
over and over
and you will start
to wonder
about your own shadow.

post card poem #2

your mother taught you
that you were wild
but she probably meant
that you were the wind
and that maybe you would hurt
someone
only to be hurt
in return
but tell yourself this
that apologies never cut
as badly as they heal
and there is beauty
in putting yourself together again
just as love
can be found
from a hospital bed.

they come in threes

it is no coincidence
that you gag
on apologies –
the radio
skips on her name
and all
of the butterflies
in your stomach
died
at the same time.

driftwoods

the day I met
Devon
she was dragging driftwood
down the beach
while I
was collecting seashells
on a shoreline
made of stars
that were just waiting
to be born.

and she told me
that she had been here before –
waiting for a boy
to wash up
from the ocean.

I told her
that I found her name
in a conch shell
and that I hoped
she could hear mine.

months after
we finally stopped speaking
she found me there
sitting alone
on the beach
and she screamed at me
about everything –
about how I never learned

to lighten up or let go
and how I wouldn't ever just listen
anymore.

so I held a conch shell
up to my ear
and told her,
I could still hear her name.

call me after you put the pen down

The first time
we slept together
you told me to make you
into a poem.

the last time
we fucked each other
you asked me to stop
writing about you.

the scariest thing
about all of this
is that I am not sure
why it was easier
to write about you
after the break up
and I'm wondering
what that says
about us.

houses

I have found
open windows
in souls
that I was too
afraid to touch
and I have lain
rotten hands
on lattices
too gentle
for someone like me
and I am not sure
which was worse.

(I never felt more pure
than with your dirty hands
wrapped tight round my throat
and I can see why
people say there is
perfection
in loving a disease.)

looking and staring

she reminded me
of car crashes
and sunsets.

she was
everything
that made me
stop to stare
and I am wondering
how to tell her.

it gets better or other various lies

a man told me
he used to tell women
that he never believed
in angels
until he kissed the woman
with broken wings.

I told him
that I never
trusted redemption
until the man
living in hell
taught me
how to smile.

the angel on fifth avenue

I read her letters
in a church today
to see if God
could catch her lying
where I couldn't.

It was like
sending letters
to myself.

I knew I would get
a response
but it came
from a priest
or preacher
not from God
and I learned
to look for him
outside of church.

rooms

imagine
that you wake up
in a room
with no exits
no doors or
windows
and it is filled
with all
of the versions
of yourself
from all of the times
that someone
could have loved you
but didn't
and without looking up
you realize
why you are there.

death

I keep kissing strangers
hoping to taste you
but the same thing
always happens.

I end up
breathing in death –
broken promises –
and exchanging my tongue
for checks
that their
other boyfriends
never cashed in.

man,
she's got problems
but so did Mary.

it was immaculate.

I am made of bruises and broken promises

I pick up
the telephone
and the sound
of my voice cracking
the first time
I begged someone
to stay with me
plays through the receiver
and I realize
that it didn't
feel poetic.

it felt like drowning
three feet from shore.

open them open them open them

you find
your hands
shaking
at night
when you are
alone
and you are not
sure if it
is from
holding on
too tightly
or if your body
is struggling
to open those palms
you fought so hard
to keep closed.

it was in the name

I keep
saying your name
hoping
that it will stop
sounding like a car crash
and start sounding
like an ambulance
on its way
to save me.

while you
keep saying my name
like it is an abortion
that you cannot
wait to have.

so I replaced
blood with ink
and arteries
with blank pages
because I realized
that my body
could never
make you ache
the way
my pen would
and I just want
you to feel it
the way I felt it.

pups

one day
while traveling
from Virginia
to nowhere, Texas
my friends
and I
saw a dog
left out
on the side of the road
and they mentioned
that the pup
must never have been loved
that the owners
must have hated him
and I was
explaining to them
how people
can abandon something
that they love
and I almost
said your name.

broken windows and busted down doors

you and I
were having such
a lovely conversation until
you asked about
the empty houses
that you
found in my chest
and I told you
it was because Romance
jumped out the window
when Insecurity
walked in
and I am scared
that if I don't keep
the doors locked
someone else
might break in.

they always come in threes

it is no coincidence
that you gag
on all of your apologies
the radio
skips on her name
and all
of the butterflies
stuck
in your stomach
died
at the same time.

your spine was a worn out page

today
I started reading
the book
that you left me
and found it
filled
with all of the words
that I said to you
but never could mean
and at the bottom
of the last page
in the last chapter,
I broke down –
crying –
because
the last picture
in the entire book
was the first poem
I ever wrote
for you.

"you were a lightning storm
and I was the tallest tree
I always knew
your every touch
would set me aflame
but I still reached for you
and you set me on fire
and it was okay."

there are only a few pages left

when your lover
asks you why
you are so closed off –
tell them
about the book
that you keep
stuck in your chest
and how
so many people
ripped chapters
out of your flesh
that you are now afraid
that your spine
might fall apart
if you move on
to the next chapter.

tell them
about how
you stopped checking
for monsters
inside of the closet
once you
started letting them
sleep in your bed.

text messages and driving devices

I started deleting
all of your messages
because when
I went through them
I realized –
your excuses
were more convenient
than any technology
and the things
that you didn't say
said more about you
than your apologies
every would.

you were too busy
taking drives down hills
to brake
for the crash.

I have kissed broken fingers and there was nothing poetic about it

your bone structure
didn't scream 'fuck me' –
it screamed 'HELP ME'
and that night
you shattered your wrist
on the bathroom wall
I think you
broke my heart
along with the wall.

you were scattering shards
of your own reflection
when I finally
kicked in the door
and nothing
was more beautiful
than the look
that you gave me
when I finally walked in –
it was laden
with hope and fear
while brimming over
with love
for anyone
who would just show up
when you needed them.

your hand
was a wedding

of red ligaments
and white bones
meeting the same oxygen
that you had trouble
breathing.

you asked me
to hold you
like you wouldn't
break into pieces.

that was when I knew
that you were so desperate
to feel loved
because I knew
that the soft touch
of my finger
down your spine
would make the empty buildings
inside of your chest
fill
with things
that they no longer
could remember.

you asked me
to fuck you
right there – on the floor.

broken wrist –
shattered hand and all.

we took you
to the hospital
but not until afterwards.

wisdom and false teeth

quit dropping
'I love you'
in warzones
and in churches.

there have been
enough bombs
inside of both.

there is no reason
for you
to look for
extra casualties
in the blast zone.

sometimes it is in the soft laughter of denial

sometimes I believe
that I have too many
jagged little edges
to ever be soft
to ever fit in
with relationships
friendships
or even
personal decisions.

every time
a person gets close
I start to chew
on pieces of them
inbetween
hugs –
kisses –
sex.

I end up
despising their laugh
and their quirks
will make my jaw
lock up.

the words
that they spew
require my hands
to form fists inside
of my leather jacket
to keep myself
from myself.

exit plans

lately
I keep finding
that stairs
collapse beneath my feet
and bridges
just seem to
crumble
under my heavy footfalls
while
all of the highways
leading me outside of town
are closed off
covered with dead-ends
and spray-painted
with your name.

and I never
thought that you
could be
all of these obstacles
that I just can't
quite get over
but here you are
stopping me
from skipping town
and moving on.

here you are once again
teaching my feet
the same thing
you already taught
every other part of me
and I guess
my brain
is just catching up
to the fact
that I can't break
all of these chains
without breathing.

wine drunk

I saw
the madness
stuck in her eyes
reflect
the attraction
deep in my cup
and drank deeply
of both.

because
what can I fear
when love
goes down smooth
and the woman
you are with
asks you
for a second round?

it tasted
like wisdom
and we drank it
like wine
while fucking
for hours
on a balcony
over a busy street
while people clapped.

thorns

tell your love
the truth for once –
that there are
pieces of you
that have been missing
for such a long time
that you had forgotten
that they were gone
until your lover
tried to put hands
on the jagged
edges of your thoughts
and only
touched silence.

we are all
finding pieces
in park benches
and churches –
wine bottles
and confessionals.

it is in
the soft affections
of your first love.

it is in
your grandfather
saying he loves you
right before he dies.

it can be found
in the writing
of sad people
with no other choice.

riverbeds

an old man says,
you sank me
to the bottom of the river
with rusted anchors
hand-crafted
out of your ex-lovers
broken promises
all chained together
to moor everything
that I ever tried
to be
with everything
that they
weren't.

my lungs
are filling with secrets
hoping
that they will substitute
for oxygen –
for you –
for support.

but I drowned.

I drowned under the weight
of everyone's disappointment.

untitled #3

my father
taught me the truth –
that if you repeat something
over and over
often enough
it will eventually
lose all of its meaning.

it loses its power.

you forget
the actual words
and you just hear
the noises.

I started trying this
with anniversary dates
in coffee shops
and in bars
or wherever
I found myself alone.

lately,
this hasn't been enough.

my chest
is threatening me
with cave-ins
and my arteries
are filling with broken glass.

I am chock full
of promises
that you never
intended to keep.

so I sat down
in my room
and practiced
on your name.

phone calls

imagine
that you wake up
tomorrow
in a quiet room
filled
with all of the pieces
that you have stolen
from people
that thought you loved them
and ask yourself,
how many
of those pieces
did you end up breaking?

the dust
will fall between your fingers
finer than any sand.

you
were only given
two hands
you simply cannot
hold on to the past,
the future
and the present.

I fucked in a church service

when your new lover
asks you
about the tattoo
of my hands
you have
on your inner thighs
be sure
to tell him the truth.

that sin
doesn't wash off
and ink
dries far too fast
for you to forget.

tell him
I etched my name
in a story of orgasms
that you won't forget
and when you feel
his hands
press up
against your thighs
it will be my name
that you feel
inside of you.

I'll make bibles
of your legs
and read you
scriptures
from between them
you'll never
find religion
as fast again.

church pews

when you
see her arms
they will have
rows upon rows
of scarred flesh
still bleeding questions
even after
the answers ran dry.

these
are her church pews
in a cathedral
of her own body
begging for you
to sit down
and listen
to her stories.

they
will be uniform
in a way
that your mind
will not comprehend.

these
are places of worship
placed on a body
more beautiful
than any metaphor
poets can write.

you will not ask her
why she did this
with anger in your voice –
the outrage in your tone
lighting candles of shame
in the cathedrals she made.

you will ask her why
with the soft caresses

of your fingertips
over her scar tissue.

you will allow her answer
to be a silent prayer
to her own body.

you will also
allow her sentences
to form confessions
behind the priestly screen
of a pitch-black room.

this
will also
be a prayer
but it will also
be a ceremony
that she is allowing
you
to take place in.

do not
shake her faith
in everything else
by bringing
the demons
in your tongue
to bed
with the misguided awe
of her angels
sitting out there
on the church pews
made of scars.

do not
be afraid for her.

simply sit down.

attend her church
services
and do not worry
for her any longer.

her demons
fled the night
she placed
the church pews in.

untitled #4

stop
treating your wrists
as if they
will bloom secrets
that will help you
understand the world.

veins
do not hold answers
they hold questions.

arteries
do not hold lovers
they have neighbors
with shuttered windows
and locked front-doors.

no one
will help you
if you find yourself
alone at night –
screaming
into the street
for help
in a world
where wolves
always eat more
than their fair share.

they
will only hear
the bleating
of sheep.

trees and grand canyons

seven years ago
I scratched our names
on a pine tree
out
at the Grand Canyon.

I came back
this year
to see
if I could find
our names.

I found the tree
but didn't like
the rest of it.

my name
was still there
and your name
was gone.

it seems
that even time
has forgotten
that we
were together.

resurrections and birds

you smoked
so many cigarettes
on the night
that we finally
called everything
to an end
and I could
never figure out
why
since you
had quit smoking
but now
I realize
you were a phoenix
saving ashes
for your own
resurrection.

so I find myself
reading between the lines
of every poem you wrote me
because the only time
you ever thought of me
was somewhere
in the middle of –
did I lock the door?
and –
are the lights off?

you see
you taught me
how it felt
to be trapped
inbetween afterthoughts
so I'm straining
to catch notations
in the margins
because I cannot find
any part of me
in your poetry.

road trips

I used to believe
that we were
so close
but lately
you've been flirting
with distance
and I'm starting
to get scared
because all of these
long distance phone calls
are to places
inside of people
that I've never heard of.

and I forgive you
for all of those
road-ways out of town
that you keep searching for
even though
you treat anything
that leads you out
from our home
as a salvation.

even dead ends.

why don't you tell us the truth?

you felt safer
holding road maps
than my hands
and a full tank of gas
came filled
with an excuse
for every gallon
because
you can go anywhere
on a full tank of gas.

you cannot be

the oil leak
and the mechanic.

you cannot
tear engines apart
while putting them
back together.

it's driving me
insane.

stories and truth are the same thing

the hardest part
of letting go
of you
was teaching my hands
that they
didn't need
to fight
to hold things
that everything
won't fall
out of them
without reason.

that my hands
are strong enough
to hold people
and that I trust
my hands
to hold them
tightly enough
to apologize
without words
even if I break
every bone
in my body
trying to do so.

religion

I broke
my identity
at the altar
of your body
before realizing
that sacrificial lambs
get eaten
not fucked.

and there are days
so cold
and so lonely
that I will
turn a lamp on
for heat's company.

so I threw your name
out of
the sixth floor window
hoping
the wind would carry you
far away from me.

theft

the only things
I ever stole from you
were glances
when I knew
that you were looking
and even those
I tried giving back.

coffee house blues

I wrote my name
on a coffee cup today
hoping to hear
someone say my name
the way you used to
when you
were looking for me.

so I write your name
at the bottom
of every single bottle
that I can find
to remind myself
why
I continue
drinking.

devilry

it is the funniest thing
but lately
I just can't seem
to drink
my problems away.

I was never
naïve enough
to think that I could
drown my demons
but I did hope
that if they
were as drunk
as I was
then they
would just leave me alone
like everyone else
seems to do.

I have your name as a tattoo

I knew I was doomed
when I went to pick my teeth
and found pieces of you
lodged inside of my body.

I tried
to spit out
the bitter things
that you left for me
to swallow.

I ended up gagging
and gulping down
more memories of you
than I could stomach.

I reached
for another bottle
of rye bourbon
to try
and drown out
thoughts of you
but your name
kept floating back
straight to the top
of my lungs
over and over
until I was forced
to breathe in
every curse and kiss
that I had missed.

I exhaled
as hard as I could
but your name
burned itself
into my larynx.

now
when I speak
I have to worry
about it escaping
in-between words.

the bottom of the closet

I still remember
that day we were arguing
about other people –
when you opened my closet
and started
throwing memories of us
down to the street.

I asked what you were doing.

you told me
that you would find the lies.

you were so sure
that there would be lies
trapped between
our memories
and my thoughts.

when you couldn't find them
you said it was because
I was busy washing them
to use on someone else.

I screamed at you
that if I had ever lied
then they were stains
on our memories
and not my thoughts
and now
that they were
tossed in the street
there was no cleaning up
our mess.

it was too much effort
for too little reward
and the stains
would no longer come out.

I am going to have to ask you
to leave.

you shuffled around
inside of my closet
before coming up
with a box
labeled 'happy thoughts of you'
and without another word
you threw those out the window
as well.

so with no other words
I walked up to my bed
and shook out all of the crumbs
of our entire relationship.

you know,
the sex,
the drinks,
the fights,
drugs.

all of the things
you were likely to miss.

and asked
if there was anything else
you need to ruin
before you left me.

you walked up to my boots
completely silent
and slammed them
through the glass window –
shattering it
and us
and you.

the body

I would be lying
if I said
my body
didn't ache
for your touch.

cartilage tearing
through our memories.

joints set to screaming.

straining
to remember
your curves.

bones
breaking
under the weight
of your scorn.

skin wilting
from the heat.

it's a disease

you will eventually
find yourself
stuck
sitting in small rooms
alone
and unknown.

typing away
at a keyboard
no friendlier
than any other stranger.

you will see it
in the mirror.

wondering
who that madman
grinning back at you
could possibly be.

but still
you will be drawn
back to words
back to life.

shaken
but whole
and grinning
at it all.

dogs and diners

just because
I was wearing a leash
crafted
out of our old relationship
did not mean
that I would come running
when your skeletons
fell out of your closet.

bones
are nothing more
than empty promises
and just because
they are pieces of you
that I never received
does not make
them valuable
to me.

not
any longer.

but
I watched autumn leaves
skitter
into the ocean
and knew
that you
were never
coming back.

I guess it's okay

there.
are.
days.
that.
the.
wind.
carries.
your.
name.
straight.
to.
me.

when.
river.
reflections.
only.
show.
you.
and.
when.
rain.
smells.
like.
you.
used.
to.

 fuck.

17239472R00074

Made in the USA
Middletown, DE
13 January 2015